★★★

HOUSTON
Astros

JAMES R. ROTHAUS

CREATIVE EDUCATION

Library of Congress Cataloging-in-Publication Data

Rothaus, James.
  Houston Astros.

  Summary: A history of the baseball team that began in 1962 as the Houston Colt 45's.
  1. Houston Astros (Baseball team) – History – Juvenile literature.   [1. Houston Astros (Baseball team) – History. 2. Baseball – History]   I. Title.
GV875.H64R68   1987   796.357'64'097641411   87-22237
ISBN 0-88682-137-1

★★★
CONTENTS

Starting Out As The "Colt 45's"	7
Astrodome Opens New Era In Baseball	8
More Stars Of The Sixties	12
The Seventies Bring Changes	15
More Shake-ups, More Wins	16
Houston Becomes A Contender in '79	19
Richard & Ryan Lead Astros To Championship Series	23
The Big Strike And Playoff Series Of '81	30
Rough Road Ahead	33
Champs Again in '86	41
Boot Camp, 1987	45

COVER PHOTO
The man with the blazing fastball—Nolan Ryan—in the 19th year of his major league career.

PHOTO SPREAD (PAGE 2/3)
Craig Reynolds raps a liner into left in '86, the year he shared shortstop duties with Dickie Thon.

It took the Houston Astros less than 20 years to rise from a rookie franchise to one of the biggest powers in major league baseball. They are still looking for their first National League pennant, and their first World Series appearance, but they've shown that they won't be denied much longer.

They were the champs of the N.L. West Division in 1980, '81 and '86. Now, the Houston Astros are yearning for a World Championship. This is their story.

Starting Out As The "Colt 45's"

Pennant fever began in Houston on April 10, 1962. Back then, the team was called the Houston Colt 45's. Bobby Shantz pitched an 11-2 win over Don Cardwell and the Chicago Cubs. The fans rejoiced!

There would be 64 more wins that year for the Colt 45's, under manager Harry Craft. The team was playing in the old Colt Stadium at the time, and pitching was the key to their winning style.

Bob Bruce tossed a 2-0 one-hitter over the Cincinnati Reds on April 26, 1963. Just 21 days later, Don Nottebart found an even better groove, no-hitting the Philadelphia Phillies, 4-1.

The leading ace for the Colt 45's in '63 was Dick Farrell. He won 14 games. The entire pitching staff accounted for 16 shutouts — a club record for the next nine years.

During the next season, Ken Johnson made history by becoming the first pitcher ever to lose a nine-inning no-hitter. The date was April 23, 1964. Johnson, up against his former Cincinnati teammates, had a 0-0, no-hitter going. In the top of the ninth, Rose bunted

1962
Houston enters the league as the Colt 45's and finishes eighth with Manager Harry Craft at the helm.

PHOTO
Rusty Staub ripped off the longest Houston hitting streak in 1965-67.

7

**April 23, 1964
Houston's Ken Johnson becomes the first pitcher in major league history to lose a nine-inning no-hitter.**

to start the inning.

Johnson fielded the ball, but his throw was wild, allowing Rose to reach second. Chico Ruiz followed with a line shot up the middle. The ball hit Johnson on the shin, bounced to third baseman Bob Aspromonte, who got it to first in time to nail Ruiz.

Meanwhile, Rose made third. Then Vada Pinson hit a slow roller to Nellie Fox at second. Bobbling the ball, Fox's throw was late. Pinson was waved safe, but it was Fox's error. While the action went on around second base, Rose scored the only run of the game.

The line score in the ninth read: one run, no hits, two errors ... a game for the record books!

The following year, Texans proudly introduced the sporting world to a new world wonder—the amazing Houston Astrodome!

Astrodome Opens New Era In Baseball

It was billed as an exhibition game. Yankees vs. the "new" Houston Astros. But neither team had played under conditions like these. Not even the famous pinstriped Yankees had seen the likes of Houston's Astrodome, a ball park where no game would ever be called on account of rain.

The date was April 19, 1965. History's first indoor baseball game was about to be played.

As the 47,876 paying fans wiggled into their cushioned seats and eyeballed the array of neon signs and the flashing scoreboard, Gov. John Connally of Texas tossed out the first ball. Moments later, Mickey Mantle got the first Astrodome base hit—a line shot to center.

Meanwhile, President and Mrs. Lyndon Baines John-

**PHOTO
One of the final outdoor photos for the Astros. Soon, Dick Farrell would be pitching from the indoor mound of the mighty Astrodome.**

son were being quietly escorted by a private elevator to the Astro president's private right-field box.

Everyone loved the fabulous, enormous, breathtaking Astrodome. It was obvious that the $31.6 million Harris County Stadium (the Astrodome's official name) would be a big success.

Even the dugouts were Texas-size — 120-feet long — to allow more fans to sit behind them.

At its highest point, the dome rose 208 feet — higher than the average 18-story building. Atop that dome, outside in the Texas sun, was a weather station designed to control the air conditioning.

No matter how bad the weather outside, the temperature inside the Astrodome would always be 71 degrees — perfect for baseball!

There were a few no-shows for that first exhibition game, but it didn't dampen the enthusiasm for those who came. A rainbow of color (red, orange, black. purple, yellow, gold and royal blue) was splashed on seats, walls and carpets. When the Astros held on for a 2-1 victory over the mighty Yankees, it seemed everything would remain perfect in the Astrodome — but the rest of the season would prove otherwise.

Playing under the Plexiglas roof that year, the Astros could only manage a 65-97 record. Manager Luman Harris was replaced by Grady Hatton in December, but it didn't seem to help much.

About the only shining star for the '65 season was rookie sensation Joe Morgan. The stocky little second baseman set club records for most at-bats, runs scored, hits and triples. Morgan was also named "National League Rookie of the Year."

1965
The team is renamed the Houston "Astros" and baseball's first indoor game is played in the brand-new Houston Astrodome.

PHOTO
The Astrodome was hailed as a new wonder of the modern world.

1965
Rookie sensation Joe Morgan sets club records for most at bats, runs scored, hits and triples.

More Stars Of The Sixties

In 1966, lefty Mike Cuellar turned in a fine 2.22 ERA, a Houston record. Another pitcher was honored that year when Houston's largest crowd ever (50,908) turned out to see Sandy Koufax and the Dodgers play the Astros. The date was June 22, and Koufax got his umpteenth win, 5-2.

The next year belonged to righthander Don Wilson. On June 18, 1967, Wilson fanned the legendary "Hammerin' Hank" Aaron for the final out, preserving a 2-0 no-hitter (his third in Houston's history).

During the same season, Jim Wynn connected for 37 homers and 107 RBIs, both club records. And two Astros made the All-Star Team—Rusty Staub (.333) and Mike Cuellar.

Harry "The Hat" Walker took over managing duties in June of '68, and Don Wilson continued his hot pitching. During a July 14 game against Cincinnati, Wilson fanned eight Reds in a row (18 in all) for a 6-1 win. Overall, the Astros' pitchers were certainly winning their share: Wilson, 13; Larry Dierker, 12; Dave Giusti, 11; and Denny Lemaster, 10.

Magic from the mound continued in 1969. On April 30, Cincinnati's Jim Maloney no-hit the Astros, 10-0. But the next night was different when Wilson got revenge by mowing down 13 Reds for a 4-0 no-hitter!

Houston's first 20-game winner also surfaced that season. Dierker rolled to a fine 20-13 mark.

But Houston's biggest moments of the sixties were provided by the club's smallest athlete. There were about 600 players in the major leagues in 1969. At least 581 were bigger than James Sherman Wynn, who stood only 5'9" and weighed 168 pounds. Yet Wynn was a front-runner in the home run department!

Oh, Frank Howard had a few more, but he also had 110 more pounds than Wynn. Willie McCovey and Lee May had a few more round-trippers, too, but they were both six inches taller and 35 pounds heavier.

How did Wynn do it? "I just swing the bat," he said. "I let the wood meet rawhide." In 1967, the rawhide disappeared 37 times off Wynn's bat; 26 times in '68. In less than five Houston seasons, Wynn clobbered a total of 126 home runs.

That's not easy, especially when you consider that Wynn played half his games in the Astrodome—the worst home-run park in all of baseball. Was there a secret? "Whenever I come up to bat, the wind blows out," said Wynn, straight-faced. "There is wind in the Dome, you know. It's exactly one mile per hour."

Called the "Toy Cannon" by his teammates, Wynn became the first Astro to hit three home runs in a single game inside the Dome. He was also the first to hit the Dome ceiling during a game. "It went straight up over home plate—just like one of my golf shots."

Despite his small size, Wynn earned a reputation for "the very long ball." In '65, he pounded a tape-measure shot off the Busch sign in old Sportsman's Park in St. Louis; two years later, he did exactly the same thing, off the *new* Busch sign in the *new* Busch Stadium.

That same year, at Cincinnati's Crosley Field, the Toy Cannon launched a shot that jumped over the 58-foot scoreboard in left field, landing on the Mill Creek Expressway.

Lacking the strong wrists of his idol, Frank Robinson, Wynn couldn't swing down on balls, as most players do.

1966
For the third straight season, slugger Bob Aspromonte hits two grand sam homers.

13

Instead he would cock the bat, fully extending his left arm. Then he'd uppercut the ball, right out of the park.

He credited weight-lifting sessions for his success, and claimed all he ever wanted was "to be a complete ballplayer, to make my money and to be happy."

The Seventies Bring Changes

At a winter baseball meeting in 1971, the Astros sent some players packing. In the blockbuster trade, Houston sent Joe Morgan, Jack Billingham, Denis Menke, Cesar Geronimo and Ed Armbrister to the Cincinnati Reds; in return, the Reds shipped Lee May, Tommy Helms and Jimmy Stewart to Houston.

The new players helped propel the 1972 Astros to an 84-69 record, their best ever. Give credit to Jerry Reuss, Doug Rader, Bob Watson and new skipper Leo Durocher. But the spotlight in the early seventies fell on Cesar Cedeno, the Astros' version of Willy Mays.

"At age 22, Cedeno is as good or better than Willie was at the same age," vowed Manager Durocher in '72.

"There must be something he can't do well, but I haven't found it yet," agreed manager Sparky Anderson after watching Cedeno dismantle his Reds.

Yes, young Cedeno could do it all. In 1972, he batted .320, hit 39 doubles and 22 home runs, scored 103 runs, had 82 RBIs and stole 55 bases. His defensive skills also earned him a spot on the "Gold Glove" team.

During a May, '73 series with Cincinnati, Cedeno took the league's top spot in base thievery against the best arm in baseball. The arm belonged to the Reds' legendary Johnny Bench who admitted, "Cedeno's speed gives me heartburn."

So much for offense. On defense, the young Astros

June 18, 1967 Houston righthander Don Wilson records his third no-hitter for the club by striking out the legendary Hank Aaron for the final out of a 2-0 Astros victory.

**PHOTO
Little Jim "Toy Cannon" Wynn of the old Colt 45's goes up for a 1963 catch to beat the Dodgers.**

1969
Ace righthander Larry Dierker becomes the first 20-game winner in Houston history.

star was even more impressive. On one occasion, the Reds threatened in the fourth with the bases loaded. Plummer, their pinch-hitter, singled to center. One run scored from third, and Bobby Tolan, a swifty, sprinted from second toward home. Cedeno took the incoming throw, whirled and released a shot to catcher Larry Howard. Stunned, Tolan was easily tagged out. The Reds' rally was dead, and the Astros won, 7-1.

1973 was a good year for Cedeno and the Astros. The team was over .500, with an 82-80 record, and Cedeno achieved many goals—batting .320, stealing 56 bases and hitting 25 homers. The effort made him the first player in baseball to steal 50 or more bases and hit 20 or more homers in back-to-back seasons.

Leo Durocher retired after that impressive season. No, he didn't lead the Astros to the World Series as he had hoped, but he did help introduce Cesar Cedeno to baseball. For that, we're all grateful.

Replacing Durocher in '74, Preston Gomez led Houston to .500 ball, an 81-81 season. Houston's pitchers continued to excel, giving the Astros three one-hitters. Tom Griffin got one against Pittsburgh; Dave Roberts had another against Philadelphia; and Don Wilson and Mike Cosgrove earned theirs against Cincinnati.

More Shake-Ups, More Wins

1975 was shake-up time again. Tal Smith, with the Houston organization 13 years before moving to the Yankees in '73, returned to become Astros General Manager. He replaced H. B. "Spec" Richardson on August 7. Two weeks later Bill Virdon, former Yankee and Pittsburgh manager, became the Astros' new skipper.

PHOTO
In 1976, Astro Larry Dierker pitched his first no-hitter against the Montreal Expos.

In his first full year at the helm, Virdon had the Astros 80-82. An especially memorable win came when Dierker no-hit the Montreal Expos, July 19, 1976. That same year James Rodney (J. R.) Richard became the second 20-game winner for the Astros, at 20-15. He finished with 214 strikeouts, a club and personal record.

Cesar Cedeno continued his march toward permanent stardom, setting a Houston record with 58 stolen bases. He also got another Gold Glove award, his fifth in a row.

1977 was another .500 year for the Astros. By now, base-stealing had become an art with Cedeno (61), Cruz (44) and Cabell (42). The pitching staff did itself proud, too, leading the N.L. in complete games with 37. Richard equaled his 214 strikeout record for the second year running; 14 of those were earned against the Dodgers in the final game of the season. Houston finished third behind L.A. and Cincinnati.

The following year, Houston could manage only a fifth place N.L. finish, but J. R. Richard made it his finest year, striking out 303 batters. That effort made him the 10th N.L. pitcher (first righthander) to fan 300 or more in one season.

Jose Cruz hit .315, good for third in the league. Teammate Enos Cabell finished 10th, but set club records for games played (162), at-bats (660) and hits (195).

April 15, 1969
The Astros take a 1-0 victory against the Mets in a 24-inning marathon—the longest game in club history.

Houston Becomes A Contender In '79

It all seemed too good to be true.

In May of the 1979 campaign, the Astros were leading the powerful National League West Division by four games, and they'd been there for more than 11 straight days.

PHOTO
Southpaw
Mike Cuellar
was the stand-up
standout in 1966.

19

"I don't really know the significance of a fast start," said Astros Manager Bill Virdon. "But the farther behind we can push L.A., the better I like it."

If that hinted the defending champion Dodgers were the team to beat, Astros' first baseman Bob Watson wasn't buying it. "The team to beat is *us*. Let them worry about the Astros for a change," he challenged.

Watson, a fine first baseman, had averaged 97 RBIs over the last three seasons. It was no secret that he had wanted to make a move to a "winning team." Houston had managed only two seasons above .500. At the end of the '78 campaign, Watson had told General Manager Tal Smith to trade him to a contender.

"It hurts to say it, but I don't expect this team to contend for the next couple of years," Watson had told the *Houston Chronicle*.

So the Astros' 14-6 start was a surprise to many, including Watson. Sure, Houston had James Rodney Richard, but that was one pitcher. No other Astro hurler had a winning career mark.

The opposition—the Dodgers, the Giants and the Reds—were up to their ears in talent. The Astros, meanwhile, had been holding endless tryouts for shortstop and catcher.

Yet it somehow came together in '79. The Astros appeared unbeatable in their Astrodome, starting 8-1. Even the road was friendly, at 6-11. It helped to have pitcher Ken Forsch toss a no-hitter at the Braves the second day of the season. Before long, the entire pitching staff was showing a 2.72 ERA.

Without constant exposure to the Dome, visiting players saw shadows on the ball. They complained of "eerie lighting" and "bizarre reflections." Fielders had

July, 1969
Baseball's first artificial grass is installed in the Astrodome outfield.

PHOTO
Cesar Cedeno, the Astros' answer to Willie Mays, hits the deck to beat the Phillies.

few printable words to say about those "little white squares" in the roof.

As a team, the Astros went on to enjoy a most successful campaign in 1979. They led N.L. West for most of the season before the surging Cincinnati Reds nudged them out at the wire.

Individually, Joe Niekro set a club record with 21 wins, while towering J. R. Richard led both leagues in strikeouts. Bill Virdon was named Manager of the Year, bringing the also-ran Astros into the role of true contenders.

Richard & Ryan Lead Astros to Championship Series

Houston's manager, Bill Virdon, was all smiles on Opening Day of the 1980 season. Arch-rival Dodgers were in town for a four-game visit, but Virdon didn't seem concerned. He was about to test a double weapon on the Dodgers—J. R. Richard and Nolan Ryan.

The year before, Ryan led the A.L. in strikeouts. Buying Ryan's contract cost Astros' owner John J. McMullen, a New Jersey shipbuilder, some $3.6 million. "Nolan is worth every penny," said McMullen. "He's one of the greatest pitchers in American baseball."

J. R. Richard, of course, was Ryan's equal, and then some. Four years younger than Ryan, Richard had a better career mark at that time, .591 to .512.

Still, there was no jealousy between the two hurlers. What these men wanted was to play baseball. So Richard took the Opening Day assignment, hurled "my best game ever" and beat the Dodger Blue, 3-2, while striking out 13 for a near-perfect game.

Ryan commented: "I've only seen two other pitchers

1971
Houston's historic "blockbuster trade" sends five Astros stars to the Reds in exchange for Lee May, Tommy Helms and Jimmy Stewart.

PHOTO
Jose Cruz scores another one for Houston in 1980.

1973
Houston's Cesar Cedeno becomes the first player in major league history to steal 50 or more bases and hit 20 or more homers in back-to-back seasons.

dominate a game like that. Tom Seaver struck out 19 against San Diego in 1970, and Ron Guidry struck out 18 against the Angels in 1978."

Game 3 was Ryan's, but it was rough sailing for the crafty veteran. Through six innings, he allowed six hits, walked five and managed only three strikeouts. Oddly, it was his bat that came through that day.

It had been eight long years since Nolan Ryan had appeared as a batter. Carrying a puny lifetime .134 average, Ryan eyed a wobbly Don Sutton pitch and put wood to the ball. The result was a 390-foot shot over the fence. Some 35,000 Houston fans gave Ryan a standing ovation for his clout, while owner McMullen laughed about finding a "righthanded power hitter."

There was promise in that opening series. Houston fans were getting pumped-up for the finest year in the history of the club.

Then disaster struck.

On Wednesday, July 30, J. R. Richard and teammate Wilbur Howard went to the Astrodome for a workout. After 15 minutes of throwing with Howard, however, J. R. staggered right, left and backwards, then dropped to all fours and collapsed. He suffered a stroke that cut off the flow of oxygen to the right side of his brain.

The 6'8" giant, who hadn't missed a start in five years, was about to take on his biggest game — a fight for life itself. A series of operations began as surgeons slowly and carefully removed a clot from a major artery in his neck; they also repaired clogged and damaged arteries in his shoulder. His right shoulder. His pitching shoulder. That arm surgery took 18 hours.

Later, as J. R. rested in his hospital room, he gave the baseball world something to think about.

"It's going to shock some people when I come back," he said firmly. "When they see me as I am now, they're really going to be amazed. They're expecting to see me on crutches, but I won't be on crutches."

When he returned to the Astrodome for his first workout, there was a hushed silence as the press and players watched him field balls. This giant of a man was like a young kid learning a new sport. Richard fumbled and booted the first ground balls, struggling to recapture his own rhythm.

But back on the mound, J. R. soon had his old groove working. His fastball was coming home at 80-90 mph. The strength in his left side was returning. He was determined to pitch again in the majors.

"It's just a matter of time," said J. R. after his initial workout. "I see the progress. I know it's possible. Meanwhile, I know Nolan Ryan and the rest of the team will never give up on this season."

Give up? At season's end, the Astros were champs of the N.L. West Division and headed for the first pennant playoff in club history!

Next stop: Philadelphia.

Critics were eager to call this the "forgettable playoff" because it pitted a team with "no heart" against one with "no talent." But by the time that October week was over, every baseball fan who'd paid attention had witnessed five of baseball's most amazing games.

If there was a "normal" game, it had to be Game No. 1. Down, 1-0, in the sixth to Astro pitcher Ken Forsch, the Phillies' Greg Luzinski came to bat, with Pete Rose on first. "The Bull" worked Forsch to a full count. Then he poked at an inside fastball that jumped into the left-field seats. That was enough for the Phils' win, as Tug

1977
Houston's J.R. Richard records his second straight 214-strikeout season.

SPREAD PHOTO NEXT PAGE
Southpaw Bob Knepper throws his stuff in Game 3 of the N.L. Championship Series. (1986)

McGraw put a rope around the Astros' bats, relieving Steve Carlton.

Somehow the Phillies squeezed another 200 fans in for Game No. 2, but Houston spoiled the party with a convincing 7-4 win in 10 innings. That sent the final three games back to the Astrodome.

Game No. 3 raised Houston's series advantage to 2-1, but it was a costly victory. As Cesar Cedeno raced to beat out a grounder to short, he caught the side of his right foot and cartwheeled into the dirt, out for the rest of the Series with torn ligaments.

Houston's bad luck was adding up. Could they hold on for that third and decisive win?

Not in Game No. 4. With visible lapses by both teams, it was still anybody's contest going into the 10th. But savvy Pete Rose, aboard first, won the game for the Phils with a three-base sprint off Luzinski's double. The final was 5-3, Phils.

Game 5 was a seesaw contest. In the seventh inning, Astros held a 5-2 edge. But the Phils, haunted by their 30-year drought without a N.L. pennant, bounced back with five runs in the eighth. Nolan Ryan was gone.

Houston wouldn't roll over, however. They knotted the score at 7-7 on singles by Rafael Landestoy and Jose Cruz. That meant extra innings.

The Phils answered quickly. Del Unser crunched a double down the rightfield line. The ball skipped over Bergman's head. Then Garry Maddox hit Frank LaCorte's first pitch to center, just out of Terry Puhl's reach. Unser scored, putting the Phillies into the Series.

The nail-biting was over, but the runner-up Astros had proved their staying power against a talented Philadelphia club that would claim the World Series title.

1979
J.R. Richard becomes the first National League pitcher in history to strike out more than 300 hitters.

PHOTO
Mighty J.R. Richard shows his 100-mph fastball.

1979
Astros hurler Joe Niekro ties for most wins in the National League with 21. The man who ties him is his brother—Phil Niekro—of the Atlanta Braves.

The Big Strike And Playoff Series Of '81

After playing 57 games of the 1981 season, the Houston Astros went on strike on June 12th. No, it wasn't because of their mediocre .491 percentage. Or their third place standing, eight games behind Los Angeles and Cincinnati.

The truth was, every baseball player went on strike. Every athlete on all 26 teams of both American and National Leagues. On strike. Period. Like ghost towns in the night, ball parks from coast-to-coast remained shuttered and dark. The players wanted better contracts; the owners weren't willing to budge.

Seven weeks later, after endless "Let's Make A Deal" meetings, the strike was over. Thus began the second half of the '81 season, which found the Houston Astros improving their league position, and even leading the N. L. West. But the Astros had one more hurdle before they could lay claim to "the best in the N. L. West in '81." That hurdle was—you guessed it—the Los Angeles Dodgers.

Unlike previous Dodgers vs. Astros wars, the '81 division playoff series was strictly a pillow fight, at least for the hitters. The Astros batted .179 and collected three runs over 42 innings off Dodger starters Jerry Reuss, Fernando Valenzuela and Burt Hooton. Meanwhile, the Dodgers were hitting only .198. Though Steve Garvey had six hits and two homers, the rest of the Dodgers were asleep in the box.

So this was a pitcher's series.

"I love these situations," said Nolan Ryan prior to the fifth game. "I'm a lot happier being a participant than a spectator."

PHOTO
In 1985, Joe Niekro used his patented knuckleball to win his 138th game as an Astro, overtaking Larry Dierker as the Astros' all-time winning pitcher.

Not so fast Ryan. In Game No. 5, witnessed by 55,979 fans in Chavez Ravine, the Dodgers made history by becoming the first team in modern baseball to win a five-game playoff after surrendering the first two games. Yes, Ryan did have excellent stuff for 5-1/3 innings. Then L. A. buried the Houston ace for three runs on three hits. It was more than they needed, as lefty Jerry Reuss never faltered, shutting out Houston on five hits. The Dodgers were off to Montreal for the N. L. Championship series.

Their powder temporarily dampened, it was time for the Astros to fall back and regroup for another season. To forget the jinx of Dodger Blue.

1978
Little Joe Morgan is voted to his ninth consecutive All-Star game.

Rough Road Ahead

Well, 1982 started out okay. At least, everything looked dandy in spring training.

"The guys are looking just super," beamed General Manager Al Rosen.

"I gotta say that this is about the best club I've ever had the privilege to manage here in Houston," agreed Bill Virdon.

Then the Cardinals flew into town on opening night and spoiled the party by humbling Astros ace Nolan Ryan in a 14-3 blowout. Of course, half the town had shown up to see it all. Somehow, being whipped that bad in front of all those disappointed fans ... well, it just seemed to let all the air out of the Houston balloon.

Nothing much went right after that. Joe Sambito, the Astros' top reliever, was sidelined for the season in late April with arm problems. Then Art Howe, the club's best hitter, pulled up lame.

PHOTO
Former Rookie of the Year Joe Morgan showed he still had the stuff in 1980.

33

1979
Houston skipper Bill Virdon is crowned Manager of the Year.

Virdon fussed and fumed through the long, hot summer, trying this and that to get the club back on track, but nothing gelled for him. At mid-August, the front office finally decided to try fresh horses.

First, Virdon was fired, and coach Bob Lillis took over as skipper.

Next, starting pitcher Don Sutton — the great one — was peddled to Milwaukee.

Mike LaCoss was moved from the bullpen to the starting rotation. Bill Doran came up from the Tucson farm club to help out in the infield. And southpaw Frank DiPino, acquired in the Sutton trade, took over middle relief duties.

Presto! The club came alive, going 28-23 under Lillis for the last part of the season.

"This is the kind of finish that should give us the right start in '83," predicted Lillis. But he had to eat those words a few months later when the '83 Astros lost 16 of 19 exhibition games, and then — get this — went on to lose their first nine regular-season outings!

Lesser men might have thrown in the towel at that point, but Lillis was determined to make his first full season as a big-league skipper a good one. Besides, the players themselves had seen all they wanted to see of the cellar.

Together, Lillis and company made their move. By season's end, they had completed one of the great comebacks in modern baseball history. Only six games separated Houston from first-place Los Angeles on the final day!

"A classic team effort," smiled Lillis, and he was right. Nearly every man on the club had found his own special way to excel. The year-end statistics told the tale:

PHOTO
The human net — Dickie Thon — completes another throw to first in the 1983 campaign.

On offense, Jose Cruz hit .318, Ray Knight finished at .304 and Terry Puhl went .292—all big improvements over the previous season. Meanwhile, all-purpose shortstop Dickie Thon pilfered 34 bases, launched 20 homers, scored 80 times, contributed 80 RBIs, led the entire league in game-winners, and was all but perfect with his glove throughout the season.

Defensively, it was southpaw Frank DiPino and righthander Bill Dawley who led the way with 34 saves between them.

There were other standout performances that year, but the bottom line on the season was summed up by Lillis who simply said, "The great ones never quit, and these guys never did. I'm mighty proud of what we accomplished together."

Bad luck stalked the Astros in 1984—plenty of it. Once again, however, the team pulled together and refused to cave in.

It all started in the fifth game of the season when superstar Dickie Thon was accidentally beaned by pitcher Mike Torez of the Mets. Down went Thon. He couldn't see! The ball had injured his left eye. Fortunately, Dickie would eventually make a comeback the following year, but he was lost for the rest of '84.

More bad luck. Right fielder Terry Puhl was benched in April because of elbow problems. Next, Nolan Ryan—the man with the league's fastest fastball—lost six weeks of work because of injury.

Then there was the craziest series of plain, old bad bounces. It's part of the game. There's no real way to explain it. It's just a fact. Sometimes a team simply goes through one of those streaks in which Lady Luck looks the other way. Routine pop-ups will hide in the sun.

1981
Houston wins the first two games of the N.L. Championship series against the Dodgers, and then becomes the first club in modern history to lose a five-game playoff after winning the first two.

PHOTO
Forsch-ing ahead. Houston pitcher Ken Forsch shut out the Padres in 1980 action.

37

1983
Astros lose their first nine games, but the "Great Comeback of '83" catapults them 17 games over .500 by season's end.

Sudden gusts of wind will puff a fair ball foul. Little clods of dirt will squib a sure double play into a game-losing error. The Astros had enough of those crazy moments in 1984 to produce their own little movie of season "lowlights."

Still, they held together well enough to finish the year in a tie for second with Atlanta, moving up a notch over their third-place finish of the year before.

"What if?" was the question on everyone's mind.

What if Dickie Thon had ducked his head?

What if Puhl and Ryan had remained healthy?

What if a few more breaks had come their way?

The '84 Astros had lost 28 games by just one run. Why couldn't they find a way to win half those games?

Well, you get the picture. By the time opening day, 1985, rolled around, the fans in Houston had evidently gone from second-guessing, to disgust, to total disinterest. Even though the club got off to a pretty good start, there were very few spectators in the stands to see it.

Even though Nolan Ryan became the first pitcher in history to strike out his 4,000th batter . . . even though Dickey Thon was back in the infield making those impossible snags . . . even though the club ran off a sizzling series of nine straight victories in September . . . still, the Houston fans could not be coaxed to the ball park.

Believe it or not, only 2,600 people showed up for the final home game of the season — an incredible fact, considering that Houston is a city renowned for its great sports fans.

Drastic situations demand drastic measures to correct them. In September, 1985, the Houston front office made some moves that were calculated to change the

PHOTO
Cannon-arm Dave Giusti was an Astro crowd-pleaser in the mid-1960's.

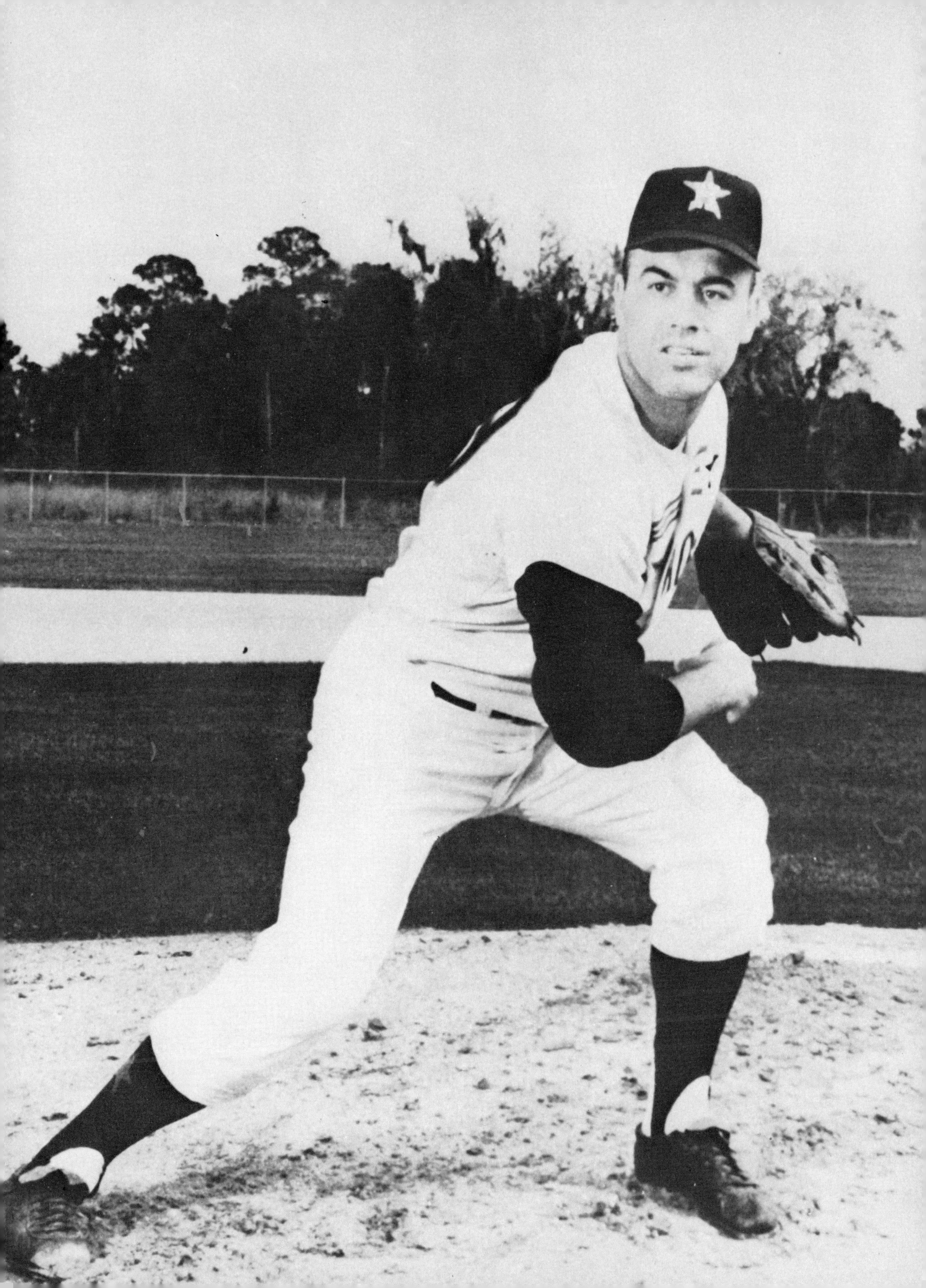

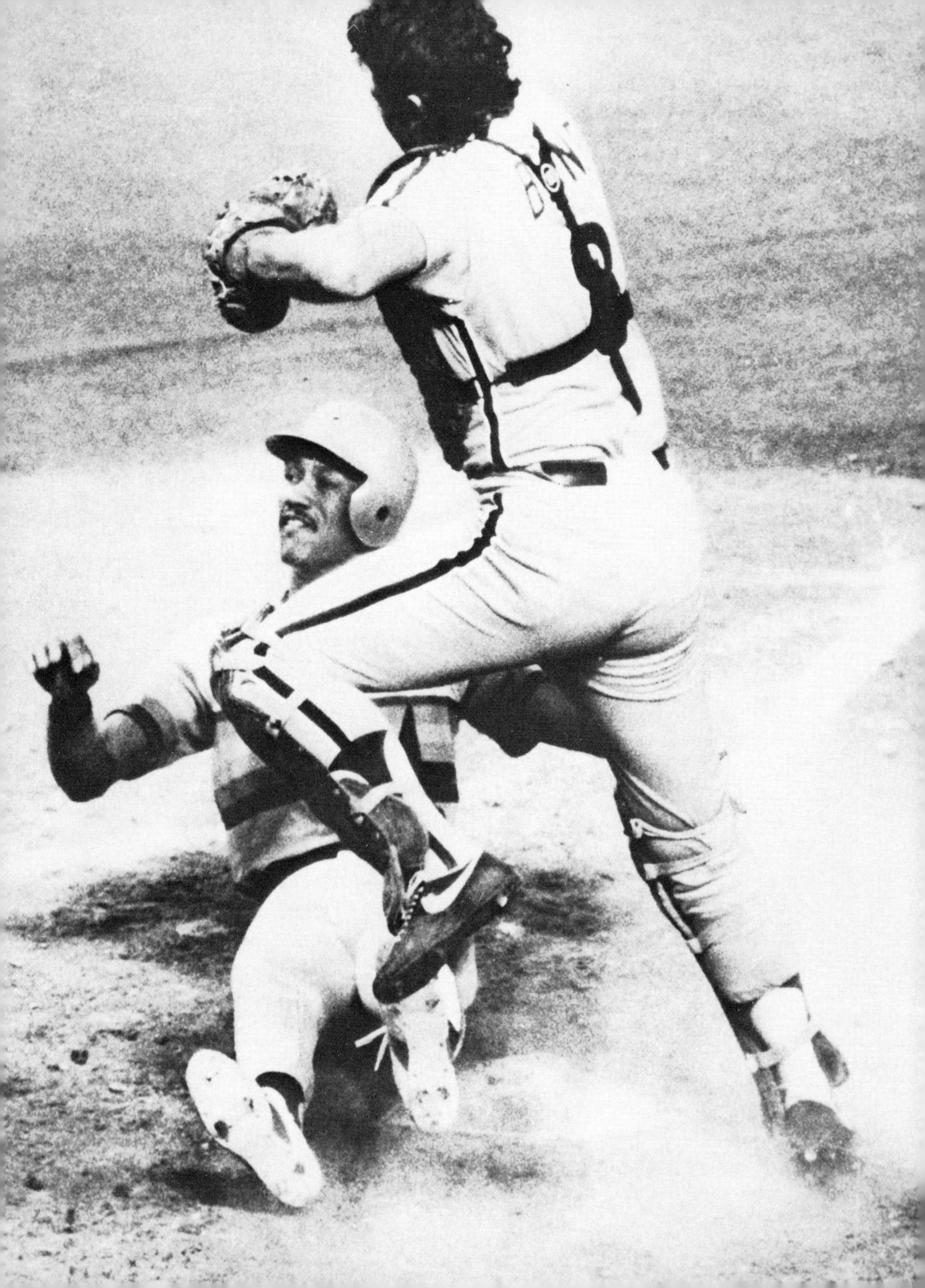

chemistry of the team and — hopefully — recapture the imagination of the fans.

First, Dick Wagner was hired to replace Houston General Manager Al Rosen who had decided to go to work for the San Francisco Giants.

Next, knuckleball artist Joe Niekro, 40, was traded to the Yanks.

Finally — you knew it had to happen — skipper Bob Lillis was informed that someone else would be managing the club in '86. That "someone," of course, turned out to be Hal Lanier, the man who would lead the Astros to the 1986 National League Championship Series, and beyond.

1984
A total of 55 Astros games are decided by just one run.

Champs Again In '86

At the beginning of the 1986 season, Hal Lanier was just another rookie manager, a man who had toiled as an assistant in the giant shadow of Cardinals Manager Whitey Herzog for the previous five years.

At the end of the 1986 season, however, Lanier was the National League Manager of the Year, and the toast of the town in Houston. He earned these honors by fusing a sagging ball club into a single aggressive unit that played like the Astros of old. Nothing fancy, mind you. Just solid, fundamental, hard-charging, mistake-free baseball.

"Don't beat yourself — that's my message to you," Lanier told his troops at the beginning of spring training. "Your Little League coach probably told you the same thing I'm going to tell you here. Keep your head in the ball game at all times. If you do that, you'll eliminate

PHOTO
The Astros were hard to beat in 1980, thanks to Enos Cabell and the boys.

41

1985
Nolan Ryan becomes the first pitcher in history to strike out 4,000 batters.

most of the mistakes. You're a good team. It's the mistakes that have killed you in the past."

The team responded by roaring into the season with their best start in years. Nolan Ryan threw fire. Bob Knepper and Mike Scott threw shutouts — five apiece. Dave Smith saved a club-record 33 games. Denny Walling and Phil Garner combined for 22 homers and 99 RBIs. Dickie Thon was a human net at short.

By mid-summer, these "new" Astros were already firmly entrenched as top guns in the division. Then, on September 25, Mike Scott went out on the mound and sewed up the Western Division championship by pitching a gorgeous no-hitter against the Giants. What a way to end the regular season!

Around the corner waited Davey Johnson's New York Mets and the best-of-seven National League Championship Series. It would take six action-packed games to determine the winner.

In Game 1, Mike Scott pitched an awesome five-hit shutout that left the Mets reeling and bewildered.

In Game 2, the Mets bounced back by bouncing Nolan Ryan out of the game. They did it with two runs in the fourth and three in the fifth. Final score, 5-1.

In Game 3, the momentum swung back and forth all night. It was the Mets' Lenny Dykstra who finally decided it in the bottom of the ninth with a looping homer over the right-field wall.

In Game 4, Scott was back on the mound for Houston. No contest. The Mets whiffed all night, and could only manage one run on three hits. Now the series was even again.

In Game 5, Ryan waged a classic duel with New York superstar Dwight Gooden. Gooden was good, but

PHOTO
Jose Cruz is caught at the plate by Cubs catcher Jody Davis.

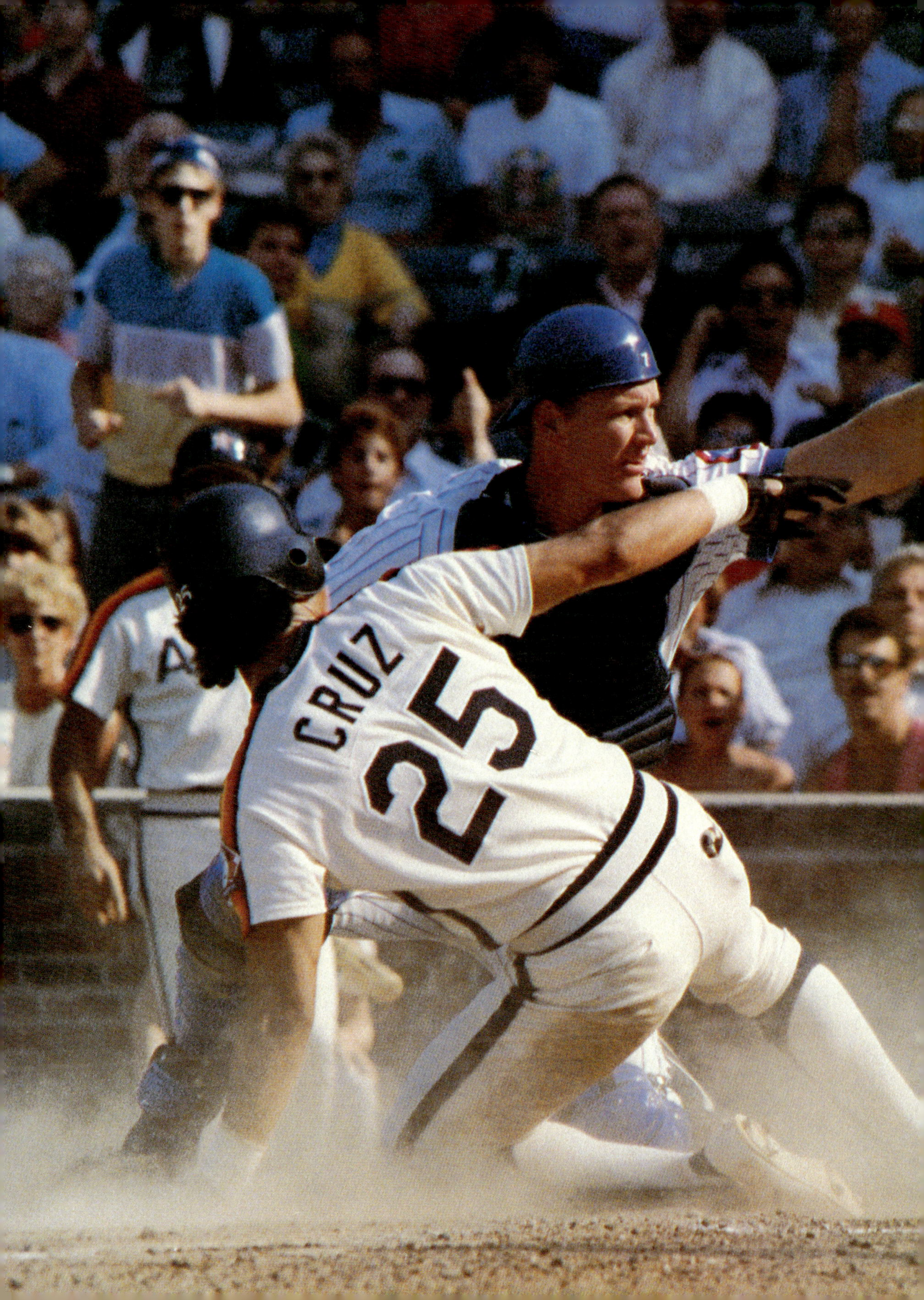
CRUZ
25

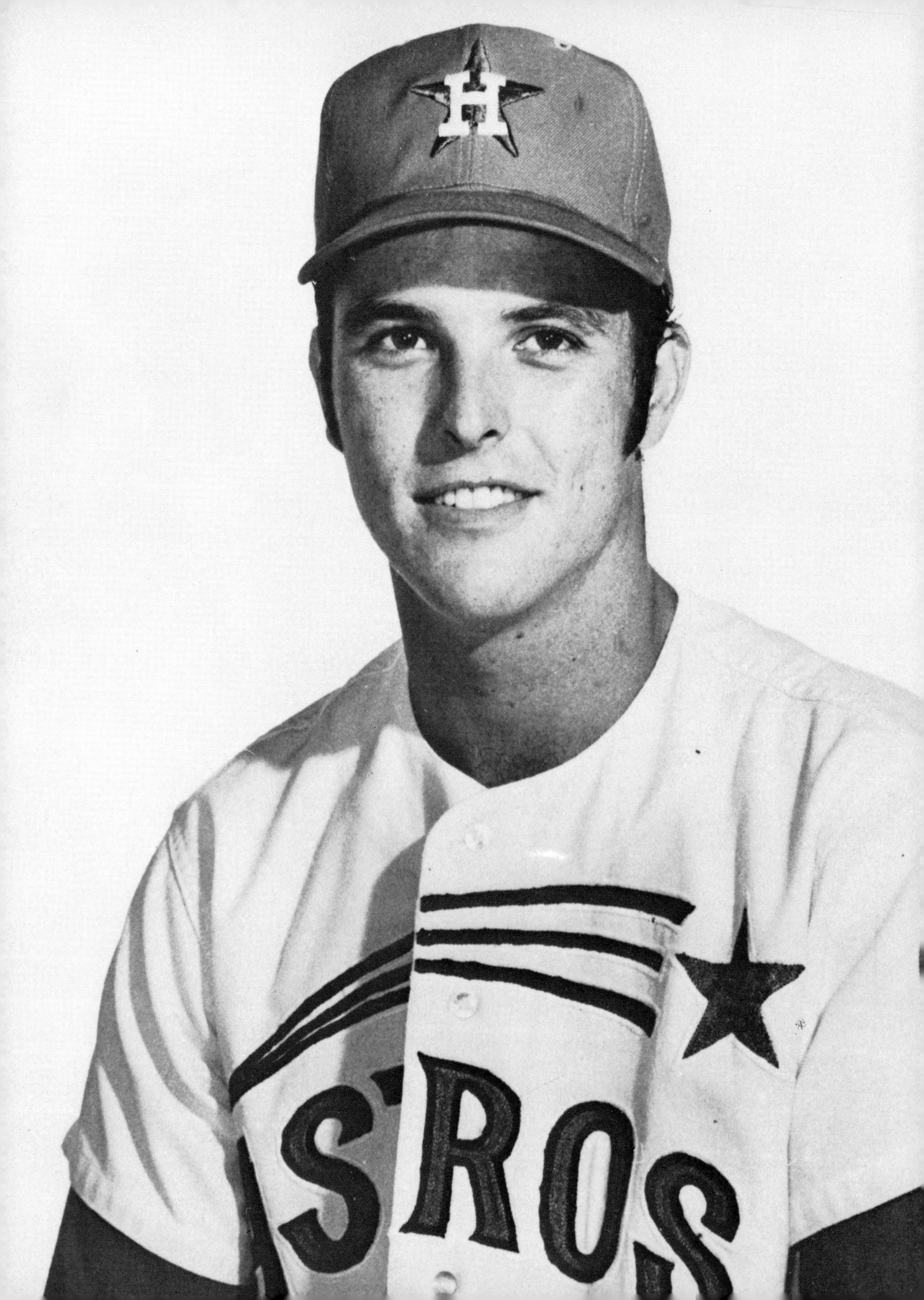
SROS

Nolan was great. He struck out 12 and allowed just two hits all night. Unfortunately, the Mets' Gary Carter drove in a run off Houston reliever Charlie Kerfeld in the twelfth to give New York the game, 2-1.

In Game 6, the guy who keeps the game statistics nearly ran out of room to write. Check it out: The Astros and Mets battled back and forth for nearly five hours before New York's Jesse Orosco finally struck out Kevin Bass with six straight breaking pitches in the 16th inning! It was all over. New York had won the N.L. pennant.

The Mets went on to become 1986 Champs. As for the Astros, they went home with their heads held high. Not even the disappointment of being edged out of the World Series could dampen the jubilation felt in the city of Houston over the courageous season turned in by these '86 Astros and their first-year manager.

"I believed in these guys from day one," Lanier told the reporters who clustered around to congratulate him for receiving Manager of the Year honors. "What's more important, now they believe in themselves."

By the way, home attendance in 1986 soared to 1,734,266, the fifth-highest total in club history and an increase of 600,000 over 1985. The fans in Houston were happy again.

Boot Camp, 1987

Could the Astros repeat as champs? Lanier thought they could, but the experts shook their heads. You see, no Western Division champ had been able to come back and repeat the feat since way back in 1978 when the Dodgers had done it.

1986
With new skipper Hal Lanier at the helm, the Astros run away with the N.L. West title, finishing 10 games ahead of the second-place Cincinnati Reds.

PHOTO
In the early 70's guys like Tom Griffin brought the Astros fans to the Dome by the thousands.

1987
Nolan Ryan turns 40, but decides to play "at least one more year" with the Astros.

Lanier got on the telephone during the winter and spoke with some of the skippers who had had championship teams go flat on them.

"Some admitted they went too easy on their players the year after," said Lanier, "so I plan to put these guys through a pretty good spring training."

Good? You mean "rough," don't you, Hal? The word around the clubhouse at the beginning of the 1987 campaign was that the Astros didn't go through spring training — they went through boot camp!

Everyone made it through okay, though. There was 1986 Cy Young Award winner Mike Scott, looking a few pounds lighter but still pitching his gorgeous forkballs.

Jim DeShaies, whose 12 wins the year before had broken Tom Griffin's record for the most by a Houston rookie, was back. Even Nolan Ryan, who had turned 40 during the off-season, was back in uniform, at least for awhile.

"I'm worried about Nolan's sore right arm," admitted Lanier, but Astros first baseman Glenn Davis said, "Shoot, Nolan's so competitive, I know he'll be out there fighting. I don't care what the odds are."

That comment by Davis really sums up the renewed spirit of the entire Astros team as they head toward the decade of the 1990's.

They play a tough, never-say-die brand of baseball here in Houston. They've come as close as one game away from the World Series in the past. But that was yesterday. For today's determined young Astros, "close" is considered a dirty word.

PHOTO
Ray Knight's .304 average sparked the potent Houston offense in 1983.